Tam and Sam Go to the Zoo

By Chris Roy   Illustrated by David Sheldon

Target Skill Consonant Pp/p/
High-Frequency Words we, my, like

PEARSON

Scott Foresman

We like the zoo.

We like the map.

I like the penguins.

I like the polar bears.

I pat my little penguin.

I pat my little polar bear.

 We like the zoo.